A Month of Meditations for
MEN

A Month of Meditations for MEN

FOR LIVING

NASHVILLE

A MONTH OF MEDITATIONS FOR MEN

Copyright © 2003 by Dimensions for Living

All rights reserved.
No part of this work may be reproduced or transmitted in any form or by any means, electronic or mechanical, including photocopying and recording, or by any information storage or retrieval system, except as may be expressly permitted by the 1976 Copyright Act or in writing from the publisher. Requests for permission should be addressed to Dimensions for Living, P.O. Box 801, 201 Eighth Avenue South, Nashville, TN 37202-0801.

This book is printed on acid-free paper.

ISBN 0-687-02651-2

Unless otherwise noted, Scripture quotations are from the New Revised Standard Version of the Bible, copyright © 1989, Division of Christian Education of the National Council of the Churches of Christ in the United States of America. Used by permission. All rights reserved.

Scripture quotations noted NIV are from the Holy Bible New International Version ®. Copyright 1973, 1978, 1984 by the International Bible Society. Used by Permission of Zondervan Publishing House. All rights reserved.

Scripture quotations noted KJV are from the King James or Authorized Version of the Bible.

Meditations in this book were compiled from *365 Meditations for Men,* copyright © 1998 by Dimensions for Living. Reprinted by permission.

Meditations 23, 24, and 25 were written by Martin L. Camp. Meditations 28, 29, and 30 were written by Bruce Fish. Meditation 4 was written by Kel Groseclose. Meditations 1 and 2 were written by James A. Harnish. Meditations 14, 15, 16, 17, and 31 were written by J. Ellsworth Kalas. Meditations 18, 19, and 20 were written by John Killinger. Meditations 21 and 22 were written by Walter Kimbrough. Meditations 26 and 27 were written by James R. King. Meditations 7, 8, and 9 were written by Robert H. Lauer. Meditations 12 and 13 were written by Paul E. Miller. Meditations 10 and 11 were written by James W. Moore. Meditation 3 was written by Tim Philpot. Meditations 5 and 6 were written by Vance P. Ross.

03 04 05 06 07 08 09 10 11 12 —10 9 8 7 6 5 4 3 2 1

MANUFACTURED IN THE UNITED STATES OF AMERICA

1

Meditate on Psalm 29.

It's probably a male thing, like clicking the cable remote control. All I know is that while my wife feels God's presence in the beauty of flowers, I'm drawn to God through the power of the thunder.

As a child, I would sit on the front porch to watch the rain of a summer storm flow like a sheet of glass down over the canvas awnings. As a college student, I remember a hot summer night when I tracked the movement of lightning as it circled the hills of Pittsburgh. As an adult, I watch in awe as the dark line of clouds and rain sweep across the Gulf of Mexico. I hear the thunder, and I am drawn to its power.

The verbs of Psalm 29 are filled with raw, naked power. The voice of the Lord thunders over the waters, breaks the cedars, flashes in fire, shakes the wilderness, whirls the oaks, and strips the forests.

No wonder all who hear shout "Glory!" To hear the voice of the Lord is to be astounded by God's awesome power.

There are times for the "still small voice" of God (1 Kings 19:12 KJV), but it will be the same voice we hear in the thunder with the volume turned down. How have you heard the voice that speaks in the thunder? When did you feel like shouting, "Glory!"?

O God of thunderous power, give me a deep sense of your strength, which will overwhelm my weakness. Amen.

2

Meditate on Psalm 139.

Here's a disturbing thought: the all-powerful God we seek is already seeking us. The One we come to know in prayer already knows us. Prayer is not our way of finding God but the discipline by which we allow ourselves to be found.

I cannot read the 139th Psalm without hearing the words of Francis Thompson in "The Hound of Heaven":

> I fled Him, down the nights and down the days;
>   I fled Him down the arches of the years;
> I fled Him down the labyrinthine ways
>   Of my own mind; and in the mist of tears
> I hid from Him, and under running laughter.
>   Up vistaed hopes I sped;
>   And shot, precipitated.
> Adown Titanic glooms of chasmed fears,
>   From those strong Feet that followed, followed after.
>   But with unhurrying chase,

> And unperturbed pace,
> Deliberate speed, majestic instancy,
> They beat—and a Voice beat
> More instant than the Feet—
> "All things betray thee, who betrayest Me."

Thompson could not outrun God. Finally, he surrendered and heard the One who pursued him say,

> "Ah, fondest, blindest, weakest,
> I am He Whom thou seekest!"

Psalm 139 invites us to prayer that is both frightening and wonderful. How does it feel to know that God knows you so well? What part of your life do you attempt to hide from God? Will you allow yourself to be found?

Search me, O God, and know my heart, . . .
and lead me in the way everlasting. Amen.

3

Meditate on Luke 1:28-30 NIV.

There are three good reasons that God's call on Mary's life alarmed her. First, she was face-to-face with an angel sent from God. Second, Gabriel called her by name. Third, the message that she was to give birth to the Son of God was enough to frighten any young girl. No wonder the angel assured her that she had no reason to be frightened!

God told Mary that she was special and that he would accomplish great things through her. It's easy to understand why she was scared. The magnitude of the message and the mystery of what it would mean throughout her life were, each in its own way, terrifying matters.

The same kind of terror that clutched Mary's heart has, through the ages, frightened many Christians, men and women. We're afraid that the call is too great and we are too small. We're apprehensive about what the call will mean in our future. We'd rather not. We're unworthy, we say; we're unable; we're likely to fail; we can't do it! And we are right—apart from God we can do nothing. But when we are obedient, God can do anything through us.

Don't be afraid of God's greatness in your life.

Lord, help me remember that surrender and obedience are my part, and any great works are your part. Amen.

4

Meditate on Colossians 1:17.

The more commitments and responsibilities we have, the more pushes and pulls we experience. Our spouse and family need our attention and energy. The workplace expects a major investment of our time. Friends want to be with us. The house or apartment must be cleaned and kept in good repair. The car has to be serviced every two thousand miles. There are taxes to be filed and bills to be paid; birthdays to remember, plants to water, pets to feed. The list never seems to grow smaller. New duties simply get added.

Somewhere in this swirl of activities, there's supposed to be time for ourselves: a few moments to read the newspaper, watch a game on television, take a nap, write in a journal, or do nothing. When I get pulled and tugged until I'm so bent out of shape I look like an emotional pretzel, I often remember this text from Colossians. I repeat over and over to myself, "In Christ all things hold together." It always helps.

God created this incredibly complex universe and holds it together. The planet Earth hurtles through space and revolves rapidly, yet it is in perfect balance with the sun and all other heavenly bodies. It is a very reassuring thought when I feel as though I'm about to come apart that "in him all things hold together." Praise God, that includes me and my life!

O God, when the pushes and pulls of this world are too great for me, hold me together with your eternal power in Christ. Amen.

5

Meditate on Luke 4:16-21.

Your life is a proclamation. Whatever it is you truly believe is seen in your everyday walk and talk. The way you feel about people shows in the way you treat them. You publish your care for your family by the things you do with them. You evince your care for the church by the way you carry out your ministry.

In the synagogue in Nazareth, Jesus outlined in advance his lifestyle and his proclamation. Throughout his ministry the words he read from Isaiah constantly rang true. He comforted the least and the lost. He ate with persons whom others disdained. He released persons from the bondage of guilt by offering forgiveness and friendship even to those considered unforgivable.

Jesus worshiped and prayed often. But it was not a worship found only in the temple. He prayed often in private, sometimes all night, but he was not separated from the rest of the world. Jesus let his life speak as powerfully as the holy words of Isaiah. He not only read from the Scripture and heralded its truth, but each day he lived its truth.

As followers of Jesus we men have before us the challenge to let our lives proclaim what our mouths profess. With his Spirit upon us, we can do it. God wants us to do it. As God's men, let us declare that we will be Spirit-led, vision-driven agents of salvation.

O Great God, I want to live my life in a way that pleases you, that is a reflection of your holiness. Give me the courage to keep living this way. I pray in the name of Jesus. Amen.

6

Meditate on Exodus 2:1-10.

Have you thanked God for the people who have blessed your journey?

Think back over your life. There have been people who believed in you, who saw something special in your life, and told you so. They saw your potential, your possible impact and talents, so they gave whatever they could to let you know that you are special. You are not where you are just because of your talents and gifts. You are here because God gifted you with these precious persons.

Moses had a mother who believed he should live. The love that physically nurtured him to birth would not allow Jochebed to see him easily destroyed. Moses had a birth sister who believed that somehow he should live. The government said no, but the love God put in Miriam's heart helped her resist the murderous laws of that day. Pharaoh's daughter believed he should live. Down in her soul God placed a hunger for life, for nurturing life, and she disallowed the extinguishing of the life of this Hebrew boy.

God placed people in your life who believed in your life—people who stood up for you and would not let you be extinguished. Have you thanked God for them? Have you called and thanked them recently? Take the time to do it—perhaps right now. God blessed you to be here, to be who you are, through them.

Thank you, God, for each person along the way who helped me to make it. I name them now before you: _____ , _____ , _____ ; and I ask your blessing on them. Amen.

7

Meditate on Psalm 103.

I had a problem with one of my eyes that caused it to swell and redden for a few weeks. When a friend saw it, he asked me, "How does that make you feel?"

"Vulnerable," I blurted without thinking.

I thought about it later, though. Like most men I know, I prefer to think of myself as able to handle anything that comes my way. Yet things keep coming my way that underscore my vulnerability. Things happen that remind me that I am not as healthy, not as competent, not as pure, and not as confident as I would like to be. And that's good. It's important for me to be aware of my limitations, of the fact that I am not self-sufficient. I can't handle on my own all the challenges and problems that beset me. I need my family. I need my friends. I need experts like physicians and teachers. I need help from strangers when I've lost my way. Above all, I need God.

Psalm 103 is one of my favorite passages because it reminds me that my faith is in the God who is able. I am vulnerable to sin, but he is able to forgive. I am vulnerable to disease, but he is able to heal. I am vulnerable to failure and despair, but he is able to redeem, to satisfy, to renew. Granted, he doesn't always respond to my vulnerabilities according to my preferred time schedule. But he does respond, crowning me "with steadfast love and mercy." So, indeed, "bless the Lord, O my soul."

O God, you who are able, I want to experience for myself the blessings you have promised—salvation, forgiveness, healing, and your steadfast love. I praise you and entrust myself to you. Amen.

8

Meditate on 1 Thessalonians 5:16-18.

There is an old story about a businessman in deep trouble who prayed: "Lord, I haven't bothered you for seven years now, and if you get me out of this, I promise not to bother you for at least seven more."

We laugh at his missing the point of prayer. But who of us hasn't been guilty of a similar attitude? Prayer is not merely a divine aspirin to be taken only when dealing with the aches and pains of life. Prayer is a key resource in dealing with problems and challenges. But it is also an ongoing relationship with God. If we reserve prayer for only those times when we're in trouble, our prayers may sound as mindless as the businessman's.

We can think of praying as a form of preventive spiritual medicine. The more we pray, the closer we feel to God. The more we pray, the more natural prayer will be for us. The more we pray, the easier it will be to turn to God to help us deal with times of adversity.

"Put on the whole armor of God," Paul counseled (Ephesians 6:11), for we are involved in warfare. An effective soldier goes into battle with familiar weapons. An effective Christian enters the battle of life with the weapon of prayer as a familiar friend. Thus, when the severe struggles come, connecting with God through prayer is as natural as breathing; for, like breathing, we do it without ceasing.

I come to you in prayer now, Father, and ask you to nudge me frequently by your Spirit to remind me of my ongoing need to talk to you. Amen.

9

Meditate on Acts 18:1-4; 1 Corinthians 9:12-18.

I know very few people who really love their work," a friend said while complaining about his own job. Actually, I do know a number of such people. Yet I also know many who would rate their work as satisfactory but certainly not the most thrilling part of their lives. And I know many who would change their jobs in a minute if a good opportunity arose.

How do you suppose Paul, Aquila, and Priscilla felt about making tents to support themselves? Would they have preferred to use that time to preach and teach? Perhaps. But the work had a purpose other than mere support. In his letter to the Corinthians, Paul pointed out that he worked so there would be no "obstacle in the way of the gospel of Christ" (1 Corinthians 9:12). He wanted no one to claim that he was profiting from his preaching.

Clearly, work was part of Paul's ministry. And that is a Christian way to view work. Your work may be stressful. Your boss may be insufferable. You may be underpaid and overworked. Even so, think of your work as part of your ministry. One man told me that he makes a point of talking to coworkers who are shunned and neglected by others in order to let them know that someone cares about them.

What are you, as a Christian, called to do at your place of work? Remember—serving is healing.

Lord Jesus, how can I serve you through my work? Help me be alert for the opportunities you present to me. Amen.

10

Meditate on Exodus 14:13-15.

During the War Between the States at the Battle of Shiloh, a Union soldier from Ohio was wounded, shot in the arm. His captain saw that he was injured and barked out an order: "Gimme your gun, Private, and get to the rear!"

The private handed over his rifle and ran back toward the north seeking safety. But after covering two or three hundred yards, he came on another skirmish. So he ran to the east and happened on another part of the battle. Then he ran west and encountered more fighting. Finally, he ran back to the front lines and shouted: "Gimme my gun back, Cap'n. There ain't no rear to this battle!"

Precisely so. When it comes to the troubles of this world, "there ain't no rear to the battle!" We can't really run away and hide.

The only sensible answer is "to trust God and go forward." That's what Moses did when he was trapped at the Red Sea. He trusted God and went forward—and God opened a way. Notice that God didn't lead Moses around the Red Sea or over it or under it. He led him through it! And that's what he can do for us. He can deliver us from our troubles by leading us "through them."

When trouble erupts in our lives, we can remember Moses at the Red Sea. He didn't have all the answers, but he did stay in communication with God. He went forward to do the best he knew to do and he trusted God to bring it out right. We can do that too!

O God, you led Moses and the people not over or under or around the Red Sea, but through it. Help me, O Lord, to trust you and go forward, in the name of Christ. Amen.

11

Meditate on John 3:16.

One of my favorite Broadway characters is Tevye from the wonderful musical *Fiddler on the Roof.* Tevye had such a beautiful relationship with God. He saw God as a real force in his life, as an intimate friend with whom he could share his joys and sorrows, his victories and defeats. He told God everything.

Tevye didn't talk to God in pious tones or sanctimonious phrases. He just talked to God the way you would talk to your best friend, and he told him just what he thought. Sometimes Tevye would laugh with God and sometimes he would cry. Sometimes he would complain to God and sometimes he would rejoice. But always he told God what he was thinking and he knew deep down in his heart that God was listening, that God cared! For Tevye and God were friends, close friends!

Wouldn't that be the ultimate tribute for someone to say of you, "He and God were 'best friends'?" That's my prayer for all of us today. When our days are finished on this earth, when people think back and try to recall our best quality and the overriding theme of our life, I am hoping that they will remember most that we were best friends with God!

Thank you, Father, that you so loved the world—loved me—that you gave your only Son for me. I offer you my love in return. Amen.

12

Meditate on Proverbs 1:5.

When the Sunday school superintendent asked if I would be willing to teach the class of third- and fourth-graders, I readily agreed. But no one told me the reason I was asked was that Ben was in the class. Ben was one of those kids who always challenged the status quo. He was bright and creative and would not sit still for things staying as they had always been. He was filled with "why's" and would not settle for "Sunday school" answers.

One Sunday our lesson was on the Tower of Babel. In order to get across the point of building to the sky, I brought in some cardboard building blocks from the nursery department and we began to build a tower. After building as high as the children could reach, I tried to pull the group together for a discussion time. Ben exploded. "This is stupid! Our tower is only six feet tall. The story says they built a tower to the sky."

"We have built as high as we can reach," I explained.

"I know where there's a ladder," Ben replied, "and if we get it, we can build to the sky, too!"

At first, I wanted to say no, but somehow I knew better. We got the ladder and we built that tower clear up to the ceiling of the room. Ben proudly climbed the ladder and slid the last block into place. The smile on his face told me the point of the lesson would be remembered for a long time.

God of new possibilities, open me to the great Yes that you speak to me each day. Take away my limited ideas and replace them with your infinite wisdom. Amen.

13

Meditate on Luke 21:3-4.

A terrible fire destroyed the home of a family in our community. I announced it at worship the next morning and invited people to contribute toward a fund to help the family rebuild. That afternoon the doorbell rang. Standing on the porch of the parsonage was a little girl holding a piggy bank. She had gone home from church to get the money she had been saving for a bicycle. She wanted me to take it all for the family that had lost their home. I took it—and will always remember the look of joy on her face. She had given all that she had and felt wonderful about her gift. Surely this is what Jesus observed in the courtyard of the temple as the widow gave what she had.

Most of our giving, I suspect, is calculated carefully. We want to be sure that we will have enough left over for our own needs. Yet the most joyful giving I have experienced has been spontaneous and sacrificial. When I have given not from plenty but from the little that I have, I have reaped the greatest benefits. Giving seems to mean more when there is an element of risk involved. Giving at this level also invites a deeper level of trust that God will always provide.

Generous God, you give us so richly all things to enjoy. Teach me to give freely and joyfully, knowing that I will freely receive from your loving hands. Amen.

14

Meditate on Psalm 119:148 NIV.

It is difficult, if not impossible, to build a great friendship on scattered minutes. Occasionally one has an airport conversation that makes a stranger seem like an old friend, but it's deceptive; friendships grow in the deep soil of time. Quantity doesn't guarantee quality, but it's hard to get quality without it.

The Bible, then, needs more than an occasional hurried glance. Let's take a hard test: How much time do I give to the sports page? Or to my professional publications? Or—perhaps especially—to television? Should I be surprised, then, if I know more about a team's current winning streak or an entertainment personality's taste in clothing than I do about the Sermon on the Mount? Which is ironic, when you consider that a person can read that entire wondrous document in less time than you might spend on the evening newscast.

Your health adviser will tell you that you can do wonders for your heart by jogging or walking vigorously for fifteen minutes a day. Let me offer a prescription, too. You can bring new vitality to your eternal soul by reading your Bible fifteen minutes a day. And if you start at Genesis, you will complete the whole Bible in a year. Still more important, you will find yourself establishing a friendship of real depth and permanence—with God, and with his Book.

I want, O Lord, to give time to that which matters most—including time in your holy Word. Help me with my resolve. Amen.

15

Meditate on 2 Timothy 2:5 NIV.

I confess that I'm a sports fan. My first reading each morning, after my Bible, is the sports section. I used to justify this on the ground that when I'm reading the sports section I can tell the Good Guys from the Bad Guys. But I'm no longer so sure. In this era of steroids and broken contracts, it's hard to know for whom to cheer.

In such a world Paul's words seem almost quaint. "Compete according to the rules"? Maybe they did so in the first-century Olympics, but now you can hardly hope for it in the Little Leagues, let alone in professional or major college sports.

Except, of course, for the Game Paul is talking about. You're interested in the Big Leagues? Hey, man, this is *really* the Big Leagues! You're interested in a life-and-death match? This is *really* it. And in this game, you never fool the Umpire. Sometimes all of us get by when we should have been caught, and some people seem to get by most of their lives. But there's one Umpire who just doesn't miss a call.

What's more, this Umpire even knows the intentions behind our deeds. Sometimes our deeds are rather impressive, but our motives are less than noble. This Umpire knows the difference.

This is definitely a different ball game. It's no place to fudge on the rules.

Help me play each day's game with integrity, O Lord, to your honor and to my own good benefit. Amen.

16

Meditate on Proverbs 17:22 KJV.

I don't know how Christianity has gotten the image of dourness and discomfort when one of its key attributes is joy. Next to singing, the most characteristic sound in worship ought to be laughter. Not just the laughter that comes from the telling of a joke. I mean the kind of laughter that is the product of a merry heart.

And who has better reason for a merry heart than the person who is at peace with God and in love with life and humanity? If we're at peace with God, we've taken care of the biggest business of all—the state of our souls—and we're ready for whatever comes in this world or in the next. Having peace with God goes a long way toward helping us to love life and humanity. Of course some circumstances and some people will put this peace to the test, but they can't destroy it. Not if we keep the basic relationship, the tie with God, in good order.

A merry heart, the ancient wise person said, does good like medicine. Think of it as an extended-release capsule, a really long-term one. Instead of releasing portions of a medicine at stated intervals over part of a day, the merry heart releases spurts of gladness as needed, day and night, as long as we live. Talk about good medicine! And you can get it without a prescription.

I offer you my life today, O Lord, so I will be ready to receive your gladness. In Jesus' name. Amen.

17

Meditate on Psalm 32:1.

Our contemporary culture is trying hard to make forgiveness unnecessary by eliminating any sense of sin. We keep seeking ways to excuse our conduct without confessing that we have done wrong; it's our glands, we say, or our upbringing, our environment, our genes, the times in which we're living—or, of course, the stars, or fate. But rationalize as we will, something instinctive in us knows that we've done wrong. Pop culture may tell us that we ought to be satisfied with ourselves because we can't help ourselves, but we know better. We know we ought to do better than we've done.

That's why we need to be forgiven—by people, when it is people we have hurt, and by God. It's also why we need to forgive others. By forgiving others, we make our own experience of forgiveness more accessible. It's no wonder that in the Lord's

Prayer we ask to be forgiven even as we forgive (Matthew 6:9-13). We have no ultimate capacity to receive forgiveness except as we extend it to those we think have done us wrong.

But especially we need to be forgiven by God. That person is happy, the psalmist said, whose transgression is forgiven, whose sin and guilt are gone. The result is the gladness of being given a clean sheet of paper or an unsoiled napkin, of facing a new and unspoiled day. And it is God's gift for those who will receive it.

I ask you, O Lord, in Jesus' name and because of his cross, to forgive me my sins this day, and to help me forgive my debtors. Amen.

18

Meditate on Psalm 42:2.

Psalm 42 paints a beautiful picture of a deer in arid country looking for water. The psalmist had probably seen such a sight, for he lived where summers were hot and dry, droughts could be long and hard, and the land often became parched and dusty. Then, in a great leap, he turns the picture around. "That is what my soul is like," he says in effect, "as thirsty as a deer seeking everywhere for water, for flowing streams to slake its thirst."

Sometimes our lives are like that. We go through times of drought and starvation, longing for spiritual depths we have been unable to find. We can understand the psalmist's cry, "When shall I come and behold / the face of God?" For we too have thirsted as he did. We too have felt wrung out and bone dry from our experiences. We want to see the face of God, but he seems far away or completely absent. For me, those times have come when I have been too busy with my work and have allowed my spiritual life to deteriorate into mere perfunctory gestures. I have felt lonely, worthless, and deserted.

The psalm ends, however, not in despair, but in exaltation. "Hope in God," the psalmist writes, "for I shall again praise him, / my help and my God" (v. 11). In other words, sometimes we don't see deeply enough into the nature of life and events to realize that God is there in the desert. But that is where faith comes in. Faith teaches us to wait and hope, to realize that God hasn't deserted us. Eventually we will see God, and when we do, our joy will be full again.

Learning to wait, in the knowledge that God is never far from the longing heart, is an important part of seeing.

Like the deer, O God, I too am thirsty for the living streams. Give me patience, and help me to know that I shall indeed see your face. Through Christ my Lord, amen.

19

Meditate on John 20:25.

John 20:25 contains the famous doubting words of the apostle Thomas, speaking to his fellow disciples after they said they had seen the risen Christ. They pinpoint a problem we all have: it is very hard to believe fully in what we have not actually seen or handled with our own hands.

But one of the advantages of spiritual seeing is that one comes more and more to understand and rely on things that are unseen in this world. We begin to realize that reality is something that transcends mere physical existence. In fact, the very greatest things often don't have a physical embodiment—things such as faith, love, joy, peace, heaven, and God. Part of what it means to achieve a mature spiritual nature is to arrive at the point where one trusts the unseen world as much as the world that is seen.

Jesus of course showed himself to Thomas a few

days after Thomas made his statement, and invited him to put his hands in the wounds to verify that it was indeed his Master. But the beautiful thing was that Thomas was so overwhelmed by the presence of his Lord that he didn't need to touch him anymore. He merely fell down and cried, "My Lord and my God!"

With Thomas, we too are trying to move from seeing to not-seeing, or from seeing with our physical eyes to seeing with an inner vision—a vision that cannot be confused by mere physical appearances.

Lord, help me to see your love and power in my life at all times, and not be swayed by doubts or earthly problems. Amen.

20

Meditate on Psalm 51:10.

Sir Francis Chichester, the famed British explorer, was the first man to fly across the Tasmanian Sea. It was a long, difficult trip requiring him to stop and refuel at a tiny island en route. Soon after he left the ground, clouds filled the sky and turbulence began blowing him off course. He knew that if he missed his island, he would perish in the sea.

Watching for a break in the clouds, Chichester abandoned his course, and began to fly toward the opening, where he used his sextant to work out new bearings and chart another course to the island. He had to do this several times in the journey, and feared he might miss the island by miles. But eventually he flew under the clouds at the spot where he thought the island would be, and almost as if by a miracle, there it was.

Life is like that for most of us. We are constantly

being blown off course by this or that. The important thing, whenever we see the sun breaking through, is to head for the light as fast as we can and take new bearings to get ourselves back on course.

Even those who see deeply into life don't always live in God's presence. But they learn to return to that presence and chart a new course whenever they can. This is what David, the psalmist, was doing in this psalm. He had sinned against God, but he courageously returned and asked God to give him a fresh start.

I understand these words, O God, for I am often blown off course in my own life. Help me keep my attention fixed on you, and, whenever that attention is broken for any reason, to hurry back to you as quickly as possible. In Jesus' name. Amen.

21

Meditate on Ephesians 5:15-20; 6:4.

As a young boy, I longed with all my heart for a meaningful relationship with my father. Though I couldn't have put it in those words, I wanted a relationship that would provide a lasting presence. I wanted words of encouragement to help me become a mature and responsible man. I wanted and needed a strong, positive role model. None of that ever materialized. In fact, my parents' marriage ended when I was six. So, I grew up in a single-parent family with my mother as the head of the household. I had two older sisters and no brothers.

Yet the desire and the need for a constructive relationship with my father did not vanish with his departure from the family. In elementary school, we used to sing a song that put my feelings and longings into words: "I'd walk a million miles for one of his smiles, my daddy." The song made my heart cry because my daddy was not present and would never be present at any major event in my life. As a result, I determined to be different as a father. I resolved that when I married, I would be in a loving relationship with my wife, chosen by God, and I would maintain a vital presence and loving relationship with my children.

The words of Daniel Iverson continue to echo my desire and are my prayer request:

> Spirit of the living God, fall afresh on me.
> Spirit of the living God, fall afresh on me.
> Melt me, mold me, fill me, use me.
> Spirit of the living God, fall afresh on me.

O God, may your Spirit be upon my life and empower me to be the kind of father who will bring pleasure to your heart. Amen.

22

Meditate on Genesis 1:1–2:3.

Time out! With this phrase, teams can pause to regroup and refocus on the task before them. Sometimes the time-out serves as the pause that refreshes, allowing a few moments to rest. Highly paid and well-conditioned athletes look forward to the time-out.

Just like the athlete, everyone needs a time-out. I call my time-out vacation. Every man needs a vacation, and we ought to be ashamed if we fail to take at least one a year. You need not go far away, stay long, or even stay in expensive hotel accommodations, but you ought to go somewhere and take your family with you. Be intentional in taking your time-out. If you don't, you will wear yourself down and eventually out, producing work that is not only less than your best but is also ineffective. God wants your best. Call time out.

God himself called a time-out. Our scripture tells

us that God was busy creating all of the beauty of the universe over a six-day period of time, that he established a system of quality control after each creation and certified that it was good. But, after the sixth day, God called time out and rested. God rested from all the labor required in creation and did not offer an apology.

What are your vacation plans? When did you last take one? Is your body telling you it's time for a vacation? If so, then call time out. Even if it's just for two or three days, take it. Get out of town, away from the worries of work. Discover that you can breathe again. Remember, it is all right to call time out.

O Lord, thank you for letting me know that it is all right to call time out. Help me to be wise in caring for my body. Amen.

23

Meditate on Luke 18:15-17.

"She's the pretty one."
"He's the athletic one."
"She's the bookworm."

Isn't it funny how as children, especially in large families, people often get labeled. And the labels stick like some self-fulfilling prophecy. Not all the labels are good. "The lazy one." "The fat one." "The plain one." "The dumb one." Sometimes the labels come from the children. But too often adults originate them and, when coupled with the unbelievable habits adults have of talking about their children in front of their children as if their children weren't there or were somehow not human, the label can hurt.

"Sally is our little ballerina." "Jim doesn't finish anything he starts." "Johnny is always getting into trouble." Innocent as this may sound, it affects our children.

Jesus loved the little children. He warned his hearers not to hurt them. He gathered them to himself. He told us to be like them. It is a command we must not take lightly.

One of my father's gifts to me, which I am trying to pass on to my children, is a belief in oneself. Dad always told us we had "the spark," that we could do what we set out to do, be what we determined to be. This kind of labeling, of encouragement, of building up, sustains and strengthens. And I tell my children they have the spark, that they should be proud to be Camps and to pursue their dreams. And I believe that they will.

Father, keep me ever mindful of the difference between teasing and hurting. Help me build up the young people in my life, not tear them down. Amen.

24

Meditate on Luke 1:26-27, 36-41, 56-57.

The years had been hard on her. Life had delivered some tough blows. For a variety of reasons, she had never married. Relationships had come and gone; none had been permanent. It was past the time when she could have children of her own.

One day, in response to a question from her about my family, I found myself gushing forth about how important my relationship was with both my dad and my children. Receiving a call from my eldest son on the same day I had called my father had made me feel the circle was complete, I told her, and I hadn't really understood my parents until I had had children of my own.

Suddenly I heard myself and my words. Here was my friend with no children who would most likely never have children. What was she thinking as I blithely prattled on about what my children meant to me? How insensitive of me! I stopped talking as soon as a natural break in my thoughts arrived.

There was silence for a moment. "I think I can understand some of what you are saying," my friend said. "I just took my twenty-year-old niece in for a while to help her get on her feet after a difficult time. My brother thought maybe in another city, away from the crowd she's been running with, she could get a fresh start. We've been close, this niece and I, over the years. She is the next best thing to having a child of my own; and now, if I can give her the chance, see this through, I will feel I've been given the privilege of sharing parenthood with my brother."

Like my friend, and like Mary running to help her kinswoman at the end of Elizabeth's pregnancy, each of us needs to be committed to our extended family. Each of us has the ability to mean something to someone of the next generation. Whether family or friend, our generation needs to mentor those coming after us and to pass the mantle on.

I know my friend is a great aunt. What a lucky niece!

Heavenly Father, show me how to give myself to my family and to the next generation of young people. Amen.

25

Meditate on Ecclesiastes 9:9.

Have you been to a marriage encounter weekend?" my new friends asked me over lunch. They proceeded to talk about what it had meant to their marriage, how much closer they had become. The weekend had obviously been a wonderful experience for them.

We had been discussing relationships of choice. We choose whom to marry. We choose when to marry. We choose if we will marry. We choose to divorce. We have greater freedom in these matters than any earlier generation had. Often it seems we are exercising this freedom in ways that do not promote strong family structures. We have moved from a family-oriented society to an individual-oriented society.

This freedom of choice is not bad. I do not think we want to return to a time of arranged marriages or a ban on divorce. But that is just the problem.

Freedom always carries with it responsibility. Sometimes in our defense of freedom we do not give enough attention to the duties that flow from the decisions we have made. We may be free to divorce, but should we divorce if there is a chance of reconciliation?

My friends had the right response, it seemed to me, to a time of struggle in their marriage. They rolled up their sleeves and went to work to save it. Maybe more couples could benefit from marriage encounter weekends.

Lord, your families are suffering even as we experience more freedom. I need your guidance to make the right decisions in my family life and your strength to keep it all together. Amen.

Meditate on Genesis 1:31.

At the beginning of God's word, we find one of the most validating and inclusive statements in the Bible. God said of *everything* he had made, "It is good."

Every man needs to hear that word: that he is okay; that, made in the image of God, he is good. This does not mean that behavior that ostracizes, alienates, demeans, kills, destroys, or pollutes is okay. In fact, this word from God affirms that all creation, every part of it, is good and valuable, and therefore not to be mistreated.

If you are confused about your purpose, direction, or relationships, hear this clear message about yourself and about others. Since all that God has made is very good, what part of your life or the world is not sacred, or not worthy of your care, your best thought and action? In other words, we are partners not only with one another but with all creation.

This understanding should leave us feeling great about ourselves. But we should also see the importance of treating others with the greatest respect. Too many boys, and men, feel that they are not worth much to themselves or to others, and they keep trying to compensate for feeling inadequate. Some men feel good about themselves only when they think they are better than women. Others feel okay about themselves only when they dominate or destroy others.

   Consider this: you are a divine expression of God! And so is everyone. You are okay—and everybody else is okay, too.

O loving God, it surely does feel good to know how special I am to you. Teach me to treat others as you treat me. Amen.

Meditate on Genesis 2:18.

Whatever task God has given us to do, we are not to do it alone. We are made for partnership and companionship. According to Scripture, God announces that human beings on their own cannot support the Spirit of God without some assistance. "It is not good that the man should be alone," God said. If a man gets tired, discouraged, weary, or is tempted to quit, who will help him stay on course? Work, ministry is to be shared. No one person can do it all. Jesus understood this when he sent out his disciples two by two.

For one thing, men, we need prayer partners. We need to study the Bible with others, hold each other accountable through small groups, and work on mission projects in teams. We are working against God's plan when we try to do any job for God all by ourselves.

Men of God, when we realize that we are

children of the almighty, wise, and loving God, we begin to trust God for direction in all we do. The Bible teaches us that women are helpers and partners with men. Women are in the world and in our lives as a blessing from God. Women are to be valued and appreciated, not as our servants but as our equals. Partnership places men and women on the same level, and we should not allow our different gifts to make us treat women as less than men, for our gifts are from the same Spirit.

Living in God's plan encourages us to appreciate each other. As God's men, we cannot allow gender, race, or any other differences to deceive us into treating each other as enemies or inferiors rather than as partners.

Thank you, God, for the wisdom of your divine plan that puts us with partners so that together we can do your will. Help me not to be stubbornly independent. Amen.

28

Meditate on Luke 5:1-11.

When I first read the Gospels I was troubled at the way Jesus seemed to have selected his disciples—appearing out of nowhere, asking randomly selected people to drop everything and follow him. Their decisions appeared both instantaneous and irrational, and were often held up as perfect examples of "godly" behavior. Fortunately, other Bible teachers encouraged me to look at faith as a thoughtful process, not an irrational leap.

In time, as I reread the Gospels, I saw that the disciples were drawn to Jesus gradually. Take Peter, for instance. He originally goes to meet Jesus because his brother Andrew tells him that the Messiah has been found (John 1:29-51). Later, Jesus heals Peter's mother-in-law (Luke 4:38-39). Still later, when Jesus is teaching near the Sea of Galilee, he asks Peter for the use of his boat so people can hear him.

Peter is caught off guard by Jesus' next request. While he doesn't want to say no, he is sure that looking for fish where Jesus has suggested is useless. His irritation and embarrassment are replaced with shock and awe when the nets come up full to the breaking point. He expects a rebuke, at least. But when Jesus suggests a radical career change, he is overwhelmed—and now his compliance is immediate.

Peter's path from curious observer to convinced disciple shows us that healthy spiritual growth is gradual. It also suggests that this process is far from predictable and will often catch us off guard.

When he decided to answer Jesus' call, Peter had to hang up his nets, turn his back on fishing, his lifetime career, and leave home. For us, too, real discipleship requires that we let go of the good and the familiar so we can embrace God's best.

Father, I don't like to be caught off guard. I'd rather have a relationship with you that's predictable and pretty tame. At the same time I'd like to find my life overrun, like Peter's boat, with flashing silver blessings that overwhelm me. So please carry me beyond the good and the familiar to your best. Amen.

29

Meditate on John 20:19-31.

As powerful as it is, the resurrection leaves us with doubts. What Jesus has done seems too good to be true. Like Thomas, we want to see it for ourselves, to touch it, and to assure ourselves we are not self-deceived.

Even the definition of faith seems to demand the presence of doubt. As the writer of the book of Hebrews puts it, "Now faith is being sure of what we hope for and certain of what we do not see. This is what the ancients were commended for" (Hebrews 11:1-2 NIV). The things we hope for but do not possess, and the things we cannot see— these contain the seeds of doubt as well as faith.

Today's passage is for me the thematic center of John's Gospel. It is built around the story of someone who had doubts. Jesus went out of his way to accommodate the doubts of Thomas. He wanted all of his closest followers to be sure of what had happened. Either he could convince them that a whole new world of possibilities had been born or this new community of faith would end right there in Jerusalem. With so much at stake, we might expect him to begin by demanding belief and punishing doubt. Instead, he chose to begin by accepting doubt and encouraging faith.

We cannot manufacture faith, in our own lives or in anyone else's. It cannot be created by rhetorical tricks or theological rigor or spectacles of worship and praise. We cannot guarantee its appearance through relationships of unconditional love. Faith simply happens, when God brings it into being. To encourage it, we must make room for doubt—not just easy doubt or predictable doubt, but fearful, intractable doubt.

Jesus is always willing to prove himself, if we will only have the courage to doubt and the patience to wait for his appearance in our midst.

Father, help me to see my doubts as blessings, a rich mine of precious gems in which the living fire of faith can be discovered.

30

Meditate on Acts 12:1-17.

Peter was ready to die. He had endured the execution of James, who had been a fisherman with him in Galilee before any of them met Jesus. He remembered the warning about the circumstances of his death that Jesus had given him (John 21:18-19).

Most of us would expect the same thing. It is sometimes easier to suffer than to celebrate, and success is often as hard to endure as failure. Taking hold of God's blessings is definitely a learned skill.

Perhaps this is because there are so few clear victories in our lives. Most of the things that happen to us are a combination of good and bad. This ambiguity helps us accept suffering as a part of the journey of faith, but it also makes us discount God's ability to deliver us from fears, frailties, or mistakes. Like Peter and those who were praying for him, we expect to remain in prison. When God sets us free in Jesus, many of us stand rooted in the open doorway, unable to take even one step forward to grasp the new opportunities waiting for us. Even after the chains fall off and the barred door swings open, we need someone to lead us out of bondage.

Peter was planning to die, but Jesus had plans for him to live. Every day, in dozens of situations, Jesus comes to us, removes our chains, and asks us to embrace the promise of a new redeemed life. Every day, he opens the door of another prison cell and asks us to walk free in joyful power so our lives will shine with his life and our world will be changed.

Father, help me remember the words of Paul (who was no stranger to imprisonment) to the Christians at Thessalonica (who were afraid that Jesus had returned and left them behind): "Be joyful always; pray continually; give thanks in all circumstances, for this is God's will for you in Christ Jesus" (1 Thessalonians 5:16-18 NIV). Amen.

31

Meditate on Psalm 90:12 NIV.

When I was a boy, no hour of the week was more riveting than the radio program from *Time* magazine, "The March of Time." It was punctuated at regular intervals by a stentorian voice that announced, "TIME . . . marches on!" At a particular point each week the announcer stated gravely, "Last week death came, as it must to every man, to . . ." and began a listing of names.

The writer of the fifth chapter of Genesis would have agreed with that phrase, "as it must to every man." Genesis 5 isn't exciting reading in its series of very brief biographies, but it is instructive, as it concludes each one with the inevitable line, "he died." The fact of our eventual death isn't news that we're anxious to hear, but it may help us focus our lives to better purpose.

In my thirty-eight years as a parish pastor, I spent a good deal of time in cemeteries. I'm grateful for those experiences; they taught me that I do not have an unlimited supply of days, though it is easy to think otherwise. How is it that we can be so careful in budgeting our money, which is replaceable, and so lax in budgeting our days, which are not? Our days are the loveliest gift God bestows on us on this earth. Take this priceless one on which you are now embarking, claim it with thanksgiving, and use it as if there were never to be another.

Thank you, O Lord, for this wonderful day! I want to return it to you at day's end, well used. Amen.